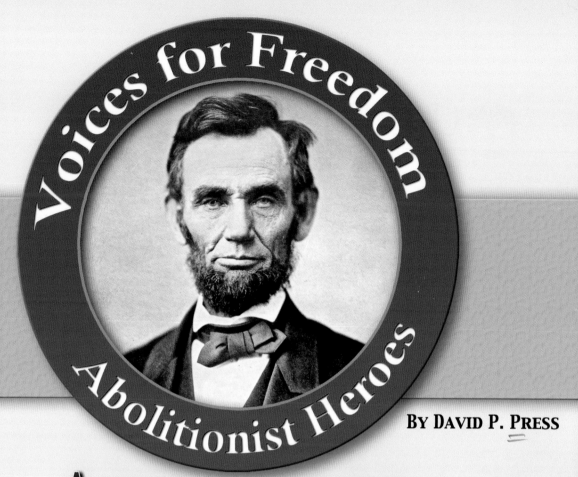

Voices for Freedom

Abolitionist Heroes

By David P. Press

Abraham Lincoln

The Great Emancipator

CRABTREE
Publishing Company
www.crabtreebooks.com

CRABTREE
Publishing Company
www.crabtreebooks.com

Photographs and reproductions:
Creative Commons: page 8 (right), page 10 (bottom), page 12, page 25 (top), page 32 (bottom), page 38, page 57 (all). **The Granger Collection:** page 28, page 29. **Courtesy of the Library of Congress/ public domain:** cover (front and back), page 1, page 3, page 4 (all), page 5, page 6, page 7, page 8 (left and center), page 9, page 10 (top), page 11 (both), page 13 (both), page 14, page 15, page 16 (both), page 18 (both), page 19, page 20 (both), page 22 (both), page 23, page 25 (bottom), page 26, page 27, page 30 (both), page 31, page 32 (top), page 34 (both), page 35, page 36 (bottom), page 37, page 40, page 41, page 42 (both), page 43, page 44 (both), page 45, page 46 (both), page 47, page 48 (both), page 50, page 51 (all), page 52, page 53 (both), page 54 (both), page 56, page 58 (both). **Shutterstock:** page 17, page 24, page 36 (top), page 55 (both).

Front cover: Inset: A photograph of Abraham Lincoln, 16th president of the United States, at the age of 54, taken in November 1863. **Top:** A photograph of African-American slaves standing in front of slave quarters, sometime during the mid-1800s. **Bottom:** A series of anti-slavery trading cards from the 1800s, by American artist Henry Louis Stephens. Pictures like this were used by abolitionists to convince people that slavery should be stopped.

Author: David P. Press
Publishing plan research and development:
    Sean Charlebois, Reagan Miller
    Crabtree Publishing Company
Project coordinator: Mark Sachner,
    Water Buffalo Books
Editors: Mark Sachner, Lynn Peppas
Proofreader: Wendy Scavuzzo
Editorial director: Kathy Middleton
Photo researchers: Ruth Owen, Mark Sachner
Designer: Westgraphix/Tammy West
Cover design: Katherine Berti
Indexer: Gini Holland
Production coordinator: Margaret Amy Salter
Print coordinators: Margaret Amy Salter, Katherine Berti
Prepress technician: Margaret Amy Salter
Editorial consultant: James Marten, Ph.D.; Chair,
    Department of History, Marquette University

Written, developed, and produced by
Water Buffalo Books

Publisher's note:
All quotations in this book come from original sources and contain the spelling and grammatical inconsistencies of the original text. Some of the quotations may also contain terms that are no longer in use and may be considered inappropriate or offensive. The use of such terms is for the sake of preserving the historical and literary accuracy of the sources and should not be seen as encouraging or endorsing the use of such terms today.

Library and Archives Canada Cataloguing in Publication

Press, David Paul, 1949-
    Abraham Lincoln : the great emancipator / David P. Press.

(Voices for freedom: abolitionist heroes)
Includes index.
Issued also in electronic format.
ISBN 978-0-7787-1061-5 (bound).--ISBN 978-0-7787-1064-6 (pbk.)

    1. Lincoln, Abraham, 1809-1865--Views on slavery--Juvenile literature. 2. United States. President (1861-1865 : Lincoln). Emancipation Proclamation--Juvenile literature. 3. Slaves--Emancipation--United States--Juvenile literature. I. Title. II. Series: Voices for freedom: abolitionist heroes

E457.2.P74 2013   j973.7092   C2013-901418-7

Library of Congress Cataloging-in-Publication Data

Press, David Paul, 1949-
    Abraham Lincoln : the great emancipator / David P. Press.
      pages cm. -- (Voices for freedom: abolitionist heroes)
    Includes index.
    ISBN 978-0-7787-1061-5 (reinforced library binding) -- ISBN 978-0-7787-1064-6 (pbk.) -- ISBN 978-1-4271-9310-0 (electronic pdf) -- ISBN 978-1-4271-9234-9 (electronic html)
    1. Lincoln, Abraham, 1809-1865--Political and social views--Juvenile literature. 2. Slaves--Emancipation--United States--Juvenile literature. 3. Antislavery movements--United States--History--19th century--Juvenile literature. 4. Presidents--United States--Biography--Juvenile literature. 5. Abolitionists--United States--Biography--Juvenile literature. I. Title.

E457.2.P93 2013
973.7092--dc23
[B]
                                2013007629

Crabtree Publishing Company
www.crabtreebooks.com   1-800-387-7650

Printed in the U.S.A./042013/SX20130306

Published in Canada
Crabtree Publishing
616 Welland Ave.
St. Catharines, Ontario
L2M 5V6

Published in the United States
Crabtree Publishing
PMB 59051
350 Fifth Ave., Suite 3308
New York, NY 10118

Published in the United Kingdom
Crabtree Publishing
Maritime House
Basin Road North, Hove
BN41 1WR

Published in Australia
Crabtree Publishing
3 Charles Street
Coburg North
VIC, 3058

Contents

Chapter One Two Strategies to End Slavery
in the United States 4

Chapter Two Early Life 10

Chapter Three Lincoln Enters Politics 16

Chapter Four Slavery 22

Chapter Five President Lincoln and the Civil War ... 32

Chapter Six The Thirteenth Amendment and
Lincoln's Legacy 48

Chronology 59

Glossary 60

Further Information 62

Index 63

About the Author 64

Two Strategies to End Slavery in the United States

September 22, 1862. Abraham Lincoln is president of the United States. Since Lincoln had been elected in November 1860, seven Southern slave states had seceded, or withdrawn, from the Union. Soon after, they were joined by four more states in which slavery was legal. These 11 states declared themselves a new country—the Confederate States of America. On this day in 1862, a great Civil War was being fought, and the outcome was not certain. Would the United States recognize the Confederate States as a separate country? Would the states be reunited as a country—half slave and half free? Or would the United States, as Abraham Lincoln wanted, be reunited as a country that abolished slavery?

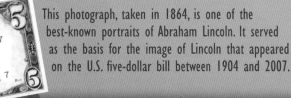

This photograph, taken in 1864, is one of the best-known portraits of Abraham Lincoln. It served as the basis for the image of Lincoln that appeared on the U.S. five-dollar bill between 1904 and 2007.

President Abraham Lincoln presents the preliminary Emancipation Proclamation to members of his cabinet in September 1862. The Proclamation declared that, "on the first day of January, in [1863], all persons held as slaves within any State... shall be then, thenceforward, and forever free."

All Men Are Created Equal?

On September 22, 1862, President Lincoln called a meeting of his cabinet. They waited for him in the meeting room. Lincoln entered and announced, "Gentlemen, I have made a vow to my Creator." He then shared with them one of the most important decisions made by a political or military leader in the history of the United States. Dropping onto the table a draft of the Emancipation Proclamation, he declared his absolute determination to reunite the states as a slave-free nation.

Eighty-six years before this meeting, in 1776, the United States Declaration of Independence stated "that all men are created equal." Representatives from all 13 original British colonies signed the document, which declared the colonies' intention to become states in a new nation—the United States of America. To unite against Great Britain, their common enemy, the leaders of the 13 colonies agreed to leave the issue of slavery for another day.

Avoiding the debate did not make the issue go away. By 1860, there were 18 free states and 15 slave states. The debate over slavery had already become violent in some states and territories (areas of the nation that did not yet have full rights as states). This and other disputes between states in the North and the South led to the outbreak of the Civil War in April 1861. The war was a horrific conflict that took the lives of as many as 750,000 Americans. Even when the bloodshed stopped in May

Slavery—A Point of Dispute from the Start

From colonial times and the earliest days of the newly formed United States of America, slavery was a divisive and complicated issue. For example, Thomas Jefferson, the chief author of the Declaration of Independence, owned 200 slaves. George Washington, who signed the Declaration, had 300 slaves. Other "Founding Fathers," such as Alexander Hamilton and John Adams, argued to abolish slavery in their new country from the very start. Benjamin Franklin was a slave owner, but he eventually freed his slaves and championed the abolition of slavery. When the 13 British colonies won their independence from Great Britain and became the United States, the legality of slavery divided the states into two camps. In this way, the earliest days of the United States as a Union showed signs that slavery would become a wedge that would eventually divide the nation as a whole. Here is how the original 13 states lined up regarding slavery:

An artist's impression of (left to right) Benjamin Franklin, John Adams, and Thomas Jefferson at work on the Declaration of Independence in 1776. United in their determination to forge the United States out of the 13 British colonies in America, these and other contributors to the Declaration were divided in their view of slavery in the new nation.

Original states that abolished slavery: New Jersey, Pennsylvania, Connecticut, Massachusetts, New Hampshire, New York, Rhode Island.

Original states that kept slavery: Delaware, Georgia, Maryland, South Carolina, Virginia, North Carolina.

1865, it would be seven more months before slavery in the United States came to its long-overdue end.

Emancipationists and Abolitionists

There were many who did as much as or more than Abraham Lincoln to bring the United States to the doorstep of the abolition of slavery. Nonetheless, no one person is more associated with the end of slavery in the United States than Lincoln, the nation's 16th president. A man who started his life vaguely opposed to slavery, Lincoln became the right man at the right moment. By the end of his first term in office, he had evolved into one of the principal leaders behind the Thirteenth Amendment to the U.S. Constitution, which officially abolished slavery.

From 1800 to 1865, various groups of anti-slavery Americans shared the goal of an end to slavery, but they didn't always agree on how to bring this about. Some of the distinctions among these groups blurred during the 1800s, but many anti-slavery Americans came to be called "emancipationists" or "abolitionists."

Most emancipationists believed that slavery could be ended gradually and voluntarily. They admitted that the U.S. Constitution did not give the federal government the authority to force an end to slavery in slave states, but most believed that slave owners would eventually free their slaves if the government paid them to do it.

Most abolitionists, on the other hand, demanded the immediate end to slavery. Some claimed that with the phrase "all men are created equal," the Declaration of Independence made slavery illegal. Others saw slavery as a sin against God, and many claimed the federal government had not only the right but the duty to end slavery in the slave states. Led by newspaper publishers, preachers, and many others, abolitionists appealed directly to the citizens with fiery speeches at town hall meetings and impassioned sermons from church pulpits. They also made their appeals in writing through petitions, pamphlets, and news stories of injustice printed in their abolitionist newspapers.

As Lincoln grew from a young man with political ambitions to a powerful wartime president, he thought of himself as an emancipationist.

The Civil War (1861–1865) was the deadliest war in U.S. history. Here, African-American soldiers collect the bones of fallen Union troops for reburial after the war.

Anti-slavery activists and writers such as (left to right) Frederick Douglass, Harriet Beecher Stowe, and William Lloyd Garrison were outspoken, aggressive opponents of slavery. They argued persuasively for the abolition, or complete elimination, of slavery throughout the United States for decades before the Civil War.

He first dismissed abolitionists as misguided. Later, he listened more closely. He borrowed some of their ideas and increasingly asked for their political support. Finally, before he died, most abolitionists cheered Lincoln as a champion of their ideals, as a man who achieved what they could not.

Slavery When Lincoln Was Born

Born in 1809, Abraham Lincoln entered a world where slavery was already widespread and controversial. The population of the United States was 7.2 million. About 15 percent, or 1.1 million people, were slaves. In Kentucky, the frontier state where Lincoln was born, 80,000 of 400,000 Kentuckians were slaves. Kentucky was a slave state, but unlike the southern states, it did not depend heavily on the plantation system for its economy. Most slave owners worked small farms with fewer than six slaves. There was not much slave trade, but shackled slaves were occasionally marched along the road that passed near the Lincoln family cabin between Louisville, Kentucky, and Nashville, Tennessee.

By 1812, the United States consisted of 18 states, nine of which were free and nine of which were slave. At that time, all the slave states were south of Pennsylvania's southern border. Yet, even then, many leaders in those slave states believed that slavery would eventually die out. In 1807, President Thomas Jefferson, himself a Virginia slaveholder, signed an act of Congress, which became law in 1808, outlawing the international slave trade. This made it illegal to import or export slaves between the United States and other nations.

George Washington, the nation's first president and a slaveholder

This painting of George Washington shows him with William Lee, a slave who served for years as Washington's manservant and valet, or personal assistant. As a huntsman, Lee was in charge of Washington's hunting hounds and was an expert horseman. He was the only slave freed outright in Washington's will. Washington's other slaves were freed by his widow Martha according to terms in the will.

throughout his life, expressed concerns over the institution of slavery and provided for the freedom of his own slaves following his death. Other slave-owning U.S. presidents also expressed vague support for the gradual elimination of slavery. Most believed that if the government paid slave owners enough, they would release their slaves in stages, and new laws would prohibit slavery. As the 1800s progressed, however, quite the opposite occurred. Most slave states became as determined as ever to continue the practice of slavery within their borders.

Cotton and Slavery

The decades of the 1790s and early 1800s are generally considered to be the heart of a period called the Industrial Revolution. Hundreds of machines were invented that affected almost every phase of people's lives, including how they ate, traveled, and dressed. Among these were machines that could separate seeds from cotton fluff, and other machines that could weave cotton fiber into cloth. The demand for cotton clothing in the United States and in Europe created great economic opportunities. Cotton grew best in warm southern climates on large cotton plantations— plantations worked by slaves.

By the 1840s, the U.S. cotton crop was worth more than all other agricultural products combined. A new generation of slave owners, made wealthy by the cotton trade, wanted nothing to do with the end of slavery, gradual or otherwise. They wanted to protect slavery where it existed, and to expand it into new territory.

Battle lines over slavery and the right of states to make their own slave laws were faint at first, but all too soon they would be drawn in blood.

CHAPTER TWO

Early Life

In October 1819, in a ramshackle cabin on a poorly tended farm in Indiana, a ten-year-old boy is malnourished and dressed in tatters. He is withdrawn, and he rarely speaks. His mother has been dead for a year, and his father and older sister have had difficulty filling the gap his mother's death has left. The boy is Abraham Lincoln. At this moment, it is difficult to predict much of a future for him at all, let alone one that will include becoming president of the United States.

A dramatic view of the statue of Abraham Lincoln inside the Lincoln Memorial in Washington, D.C.

Early Childhood

Abraham Lincoln was born on February 12, 1809, and his earliest education about slavery began in his family. For the first seven years of Lincoln's life, his parents, Thomas and Nancy Hanks Lincoln, lived and worked on their small family farm in rural Hardin County, Kentucky. Some distant relatives owned slaves, but Abe's parents did not. They believed slavery was morally wrong. They also thought it was unfair. Small-

Thomas Lincoln, the father of Abraham Lincoln.

farm farmers like Thomas Lincoln had to compete with slave-owning farmers. Because of their free labor, slaveholding farmers could produce more crops and sell them at a lower price than Thomas could.

The Lincolns worshiped at the South Fork Baptist Church. Church members were split on the issue of slavery, with some for it and some against it. When this disagreement became heated, some anti-slavery members broke from the church and formed their own congregation. The Lincolns went with them.

Young Abe rarely mixed with anyone except his parents and his older sister, Sarah (1807–1828). By the age of four or five, Abe's daily life became a series of chores and he rarely left the farm. Abe didn't even go to school until the age of ten.

Larger plantations that used slave labor, like the one shown here, could produce more crops and sell them more cheaply than smaller farms like the one run by Thomas Lincoln. This photo, taken around 1862, shows a group of slaves tending to a sweet potato crop in South Carolina.

Complicated Kentucky

Outside that bubble, Kentucky shaped up as a debating stage for pro- and anti-slavery voices. Kentucky was originally part of Virginia, a slave state. Kentucky became a state in 1792 and, in 1799, young lawyer Henry Clay (1777–1852), argued that the gradual elimination of slavery should be built into the new state constitution. Clay, who later became Abraham Lincoln's first political hero, lost that argument and by the time Lincoln was born, Kentucky had passed laws that made it illegal for a free black person to move there. As a result, during Lincoln's Kentucky years, only 28 free blacks lived in Hardin County where the Lincolns also lived. It is doubtful that young Abe met any of them.

A statue of Abraham Lincoln sits in the town square of Hodgenville, Kentucky, in the area where Abe Lincoln lived as a young boy.

Thomas Lincoln had a pioneering spirit. By the time Abe was seven, the Lincolns had lived in a succession of four rather primitive cabins. With each move, trees had to be cleared, roots dug up, water hauled, outbuildings built, firewood chopped, fields plowed, and crops sown, tended to, harvested, cooked, and canned. The work was hard and never done.

Thomas owned land, including several farms. But, by 1816, he had lost some of that land in complicated court cases, and other land was still in dispute. Tired of the legal wrangling, he moved the family to Indiana.

On to Indiana

Politically, Indiana differed from Kentucky in at least one huge way. Indiana was a free state, and slavery was therefore illegal. Free blacks could move to Indiana, although they could not vote, testify in court against whites, or attend public schools. Thomas did not move his family to Indiana because it was a free state, however. He moved there to get free land that had become available after the War of 1812 between the United States and Great Britain.

Abe's life in Indiana was even more severe than it had been in Kentucky. There were more trees, more roots, and more isolation. Tragedy struck in 1818 when Abe's mother Nancy died of milk sickness, a horrible death caused by drinking the milk of cows that had eaten white snakeroot—a potent, poisonous plant. Abe helped dig his mother's grave within yards of their cabin. This was perhaps the lowest moment of young Abraham Lincoln's rugged life.

Abe Lincoln's stepmother, Sarah Bush Lincoln, encouraged Abe's love for reading. She recognized in Abe something different and special that set him apart from other children—even her own.

Then something happened that changed Lincoln's life. In 1819, Thomas married widow Sarah Bush Johnston, who had three children of her own. Sarah immediately set about cleaning up Abe and Sarah and mending their clothes. She did not stop there. Although she was unable to read or write, Abe's new stepmother encouraged Abe to read and to go to school whenever he could.

Abe's Education, In and Out of the Classroom

When he was ten, Abe received his first formal education. He attended a "blab" school for about two months. A blab school was a one-room schoolhouse with students from all different levels reciting different lessons aloud, all at once. It was noisy and sometimes sounded like gibberish or "blabbering." The school year was usually just two months in the winter, when there were not as many farm chores. Two years later, when Abe was 12, he attended another school, and again for a few months in 1824, when he was 15. That was it.

This one-room school, photographed in the late 1800s, is similar to the "blab school" that Abraham Lincoln attended when he was a boy.

Pieced together, Abraham Lincoln's formal education lasted less than one year, but he had a remarkable talent for self-education. Sarah Bush Lincoln helped him borrow as many books as they could find. He also read every newspaper he could get his hands on. Abe's knowledge of the world off the farm, including the issue of slavery as reported by some newspaper articles, grew quickly.

In his teens, Abe tried to spend time off the farm whenever he could. He discovered the social world of the country store in town. There, men told stories and talked politics. He heard the names of national political leaders who meant nothing to him at the time, but soon would. One of those leaders was Henry Clay, the Kentucky politician who favored a gradual end to slavery and whose ideas influenced Lincoln's own. Abe also visited the local courthouse a few times, where he was fascinated by trials and legal arguments. To make up for his time away from the farm, young Lincoln took on a few odd jobs to help support the family.

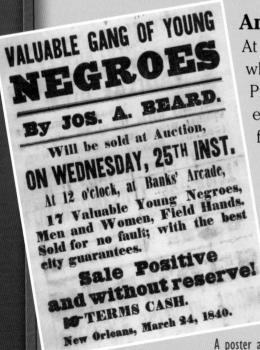

A poster advertising the auction of slaves, male and female alike, to the highest bidder in New Orleans in 1840.

An Eye Opener in New Orleans

At the age of 18, Abe Lincoln—the young man who would one day issue the Emancipation Proclamation—had almost no personal experience with African Americans, slave or free. This changed in 1828, when he spent a month in the bustling seaport of New Orleans, Louisiana.

An Indiana storekeeper hired Abe and a few other young men to take a load of overstocked dry foods such as beans and oats down the Ohio and Mississippi rivers on a flat boat. They were to sell the goods and the boat in New Orleans, then return by steamship.

Abe suddenly found himself in a Southern city of 50,000 people, filled with new foods, arts, and music. Of these 50,000 people, 17,000 were slaves and 12,000 were free blacks. People of Spanish and French descent, and merchants from around the world, also crisscrossed the streets at all hours of the day and night.

In New Orleans, Lincoln witnessed two extremes. On one hand, he saw the peaceful intermingling of the races; on the other, slave auctions at which African Americans were bought and sold like his surplus food. Sometimes slave families were torn apart when the father was sold to one buyer, and the mother and children to another.

Lincoln never wrote about this part of his New Orleans experiences, but they no doubt opened his eyes to the harsher realities of slavery and likely shaped his opinions in years to come.

Moving On

In 1830, fearing an outbreak of milk sickness in Indiana, Thomas decided to move the family west to Illinois, another free state. In 1831, he moved the family to yet another location in Illinois. Around then Abraham, at 22, had decided it was time to strike out on his own. He hired on for his second trip to New Orleans. There, he again witnessed the cruel contradiction of slavery in a city that was one of the most culturally and racially diverse in the nation.

When Lincoln returned to Illinois, he set out to start a life of his own. His Indiana years, which began so grimly and with so little promise, ended with a promise of personal freedom and a new world opening before him.

This statue in Chicago depicts "Young Lincoln" as barefoot and holding a book. Whenever the teenaged Abe Lincoln walked by, the townsfolk noticed this thin, strong young man. At a time when the average height for an adult American male was 5 feet 6 inches (168 cm), Abe at 17 already stood 6 feet 2 inches (188 cm) tall.

CHAPTER THREE

Lincoln Enters Politics

In 1831, at the age of 22, Abraham Lincoln had left the home of his parents. He moved to New Salem, Illinois, where he took a job as a clerk in a general store and lived in the back. One of the things he loved about this job was that it gave him time to read, not only books, but newspapers. Almost every one of the 200 New Salem townsfolk came into the general store to buy goods. Abe soon got to know them all, and they got to know him. Some townsmen lingered at the store, where they told stories and jokes, and often talked about politics. Unfortunately, however, the store went out of business, leaving Abe out of work.

This statue was created in 1930 and placed in Dixon, Illinois, where Abraham Lincoln joined the Illinois Militia. It shows Lincoln as a captain in the militia in 1832. Years after his service, Lincoln humorously recalled being elected captain by the men in his company: "I was elected a Captain of Volunteers—a success which gave me more pleasure than any I have had since."

Business, Military, Law, and State Legislature

In 1832, Lincoln was 23 years old and had lived in New Salem for less than one year. In March, he began his career in politics by running for the Illinois state legislature. The legislature was responsible for making Illinois state laws and for electing the two U.S. senators from Illinois.

In April, still unemployed, and with the election several months away, Lincoln volunteered to join the Illinois Militia. Militias were state military forces roughly equivalent to today's National Guard. Although Lincoln did not see combat in what was known as the Black Hawk War, he was elected captain of the company in which he served. Allowing men to elect their own commanding officer was the practice at that time. In July, his services were no longer needed, and he was honorably discharged.

When Lincoln returned to civilian life in July, he also returned to his campaign for the state legislature. When the election was held in August, he lost, but he wasn't discouraged. He would be in and out of politics for the rest of his life.

At around the same time—still in 1832, still 23, and still unemployed—Lincoln became part owner of another general store in New Salem. Borrowing money to stock the store, Lincoln and his business partner, William F. Berry, struggled financially. In 1833, Lincoln sold his share of the store. The store failed, Berry died suddenly, and Lincoln was left with debt that had been Berry's responsibility to pay off.

A replica of the store in which Abraham Lincoln worked in New Salem, Illinois.

The Illinois Old State Capitol in Springfield, where Abraham Lincoln argued cases before the Illinois Supreme Court, served in the state legislature, and debated with Stephen Douglas while running for the U.S. Senate. Today, it is an Illinois State Historic Site.

Lincoln was deep in debt, and his lenders wanted their money. To pay them what he could, Lincoln took whatever odd jobs he could get, such as helping New Salem farmers at harvest time. He also worked briefly as a postmaster, all the while reading almost every available moment. He was often seen walking to or from work with an open book, barely looking where he was going.

Increasingly, law books filled his reading list. Soon he was writing up simple legal documents for the townspeople, such as rental leases or contracts. By 1836, entirely through self-study, Lincoln passed the bar exam, allowing him to practice law in Illinois. From then on, he earned most of his income practicing law. Before his law career ended when he was elected president in 1860, Lincoln served more than 5,000 clients.

Meanwhile, bitten by the bug of politics, Lincoln ran again for the Illinois state legislature in 1834. This time he won, and he was re-elected in 1836, 1838, and 1840. Even though the abolitionist movement began to gain momentum during this period, slavery was not one of Lincoln's central campaign issues, particularly in the free state of Illinois.

When Lincoln served in the Illinois state legislature in the 1830s and 1840s, he spoke less about issues related to slavery than about improvements to infrastructure—railroads, canals, and other projects—that he wanted the state government to help pay for. This photo, taken later in the 1800s, is of one such massive project—the building of the Chicago Sanitary and Ship Canal, which connected the Great Lakes to the Mississippi River system.

Lincoln and the Whigs

At the time, the nation's two major political parties were the Democrats and the Whigs. From the 1830s, when he first ran for office, through the mid-1850s, Abraham Lincoln was a staunch Whig. The Whigs' national leader was Henry Clay—Abraham Lincoln's political hero. Lincoln soon became a leader of the Illinois Whig Party. The Whigs believed a strong federal government that helped industry and other businesses was the best way to help the United States grow. Slavery did not become a major issue for the Whigs until the 1850s. When it did, bickering between Southern and Northern Whigs divided the party into pro- and anti-slavery factions that soon broke the party up.

Henry Clay, a founder of the Whig Party, was an influential U.S. congressman and senator from Kentucky. He ran unsuccessfully for president in 1824, 1832, and 1844. Although a slave owner himself, Clay advocated eliminating slavery through gradual emancipation.

Throughout Lincoln's political career, Illinois voters were mostly Democrats. The Whig candidates for governor and senator never won. The Whig candidates for president never carried Illinois. For an ambitious politician like Lincoln, the smart move was to declare himself a Democrat. Lincoln stuck with his Whig principles, however, and he kept winning because Democrats crossed party lines to vote for him.

Lincoln and the Abolitionists

In 1836—84 years before women gained the right to vote in the United States—Lincoln spoke up in favor of women's suffrage, which meant granting women the right to vote. In a letter to the *Sangamon Journal*, an Illinois newspaper, he wrote that he supported "admitting all whites to the right of suffrage who pay taxes or bear arms—[including] females."

This opinion did not include African Americans, and very few women qualified, but it was a daring proposal that was ahead of its time.

Also in 1836, Lincoln made his first political stand against slavery in the Illinois state legislature. As abolitionist voices calling for an

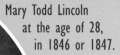

Mary Todd Lincoln at the age of 28, in 1846 or 1847.

immediate end to slavery grew louder, so did an ugly backlash, or reaction, against the abolitionists. Even in a free state such as Illinois, not everyone was opposed to slavery. In the 1830s, many felt that abolitionists and their beliefs were too radical. Mobs with clubs sometimes attacked abolitionist group meetings. Mob leaders were rarely arrested, never convicted, and sometimes awarded with political appointments.

Identifying with abolitionists in Illinois could be political suicide. In early 1837, the Illinois state legislature introduced a measure generally condemning abolitionists and the abolition of slavery. The resolution did not make or change any Illinois law. It gave the lawmakers a way to show the voters how they felt. The resolution passed, 77 to 6. Lincoln was one of the six who voted against it.

Not only did Lincoln vote against the resolution, but he filed a written protest. The protest declared his conviction that slavery was immoral and unjust. Lincoln did not champion the abolitionists, but he condemned violence against abolitionists.

Nine months later, in January 1838, Lincoln repeated this position, this time in a public speech before the student body of a school called the Young Men's Lyceum. Lincoln vehemently condemned mob violence, raised questions about slavery, and defended the rights of abolitionists. A full text of his speech, known as

The Lincolns' eldest son, Robert Todd Lincoln, as photographed around 1865, at about the age of 22.

20

the Lyceum Address, was published in the *Sangamon Journal*. It was Lincoln's first published speech, and many of the voters in his district undoubtedly read it. At the young age of 28, Lincoln's reputation as an anti-slavery politician was taking hold.

Springfield and Romance

In 1837, when the Illinois state capital moved from Vandalia to Springfield, Lincoln left tiny New Salem and moved to this new, larger city. As a legislator and lawyer, Lincoln mingled, uncomfortably, with people from educated and wealthy families. His lingering unrefined speech and mannerisms showed. So it surprised friends when, in 1839, he struck up a friendship with Mary Todd, who was from a well-established Kentucky family. After an engagement and a serious break-up, Mary and Abe suddenly married in November 1842. In August of the next year, Robert Todd Lincoln, the first of four sons, was born.

In 1842, after an eight-year career as an Illinois state legislator, Lincoln quit public office to dedicate himself full-time to practicing law. Except for a two-year term in the U.S. House of Representatives (1846–1848), Lincoln would hold no political office until he was elected president in 1860.

Dueling Over Dollars

Before Abraham Lincoln and Mary Todd married, Mary's sharp political wit almost put a dueling sword in her future husband's hand. In 1842, the Whigs and the Democrats were in a dispute over how Illinois government should handle the state debt. The state auditor was James Shields, a Democrat, and he directed tax collectors to stop accepting paper money. Lincoln wrote anonymous letters to the *Sangamon Journal* making fun of Shields's position. Mary Todd did the same. It was too much for Shields. Furious, he demanded to know the identity of his attacker. Protecting Mary, Lincoln took responsibility for all the letters. At the time, it was still acceptable for people to settle disputes with weapons in a duel. Shields challenged Lincoln, and Lincoln accepted, choosing cavalry broadswords for the duel. Friends intervened and convinced them to call off the contest before swords clashed.

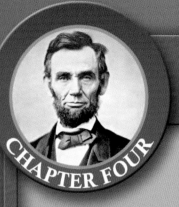

CHAPTER FOUR

Slavery

In 1846, Abraham Lincoln was elected to the United States Congress, where he would serve in the House of Representatives as a congressman from Illinois. At the time, there were 13 months between the time of the election and when the new Congress convened. So in 1847, Abraham, Mary, and young Robert Lincoln began a leisurely journey from Springfield, Illinois, to Washington, D.C. Their first stop was a three-week vacation with Mary's family in Lexington, Kentucky.

Lincoln and Clay

For Lincoln, the stopover in Kentucky turned out to be much more than a vacation. His political hero, Henry Clay, was in town. Lincoln went to hear him give a speech, and a fiery speech it was. At the time, the United States was fighting a controversial war with Mexico. Clay condemned the Mexican-American War as a blatant effort to seize large pieces of Mexican land after defeating the Mexican

A photograph of Abraham Lincoln in 1846 or 1847, at the time of his election to the U.S. House of Representatives in Washington, D.C.

army, claim that land as U.S. territory, and make it available for the expansion of slavery—all of which was backed by pro-slavery forces.

This map shows, in white, land that was once a part of Mexico and became ceded, or given up, to the United States around and after the time of the Mexican-American War (1846–1848). This new U.S. territory was a potential battleground between pro- and anti-slavery forces.

Clay's speech reawakened Lincoln's anti-slavery feelings. Yet Clay was not an abolitionist. Despite his strong condemnation of slavery, Clay still wanted to see it end gradually, and he wanted to assure white Americans that freed slaves would go to West Africa and live in a new country called Liberia. This part of his argument was known as "colonization."

Some supporters of colonization feared that freed blacks would incite enslaved African Americans to rise up against their masters, or they didn't want to grant equal rights to black people. Others, such as Henry Clay, were opposed to slavery but felt that blacks could never be fully integrated into a deeply prejudiced U.S. society. Thus, Clay argued, it would be better for them to "resettle" in Africa. Lincoln, at least for the time being, adopted Clay's views on slavery as his own.

Clay and other emancipationists believed the U.S. Constitution did not permit the federal government to abolish slavery in the states. The territories and the nation's capital, Washington, D.C., were a different story. They were federal lands and were not a part of any state. So slavery in Washington, D.C., became a battleground of debate. If the emancipationist politicians passed laws to abolish slavery in the nation's capital, it would strike a blow against pro-slavery forces.

Mr. Lincoln Goes to Washington

So, where did newly elected Congressman Lincoln stand on these issues? He never said he believed the Mexican-American War was a ploy to expand slavery. In his first speech in Congress, however, Lincoln accused President James K. Polk of lying to the U.S. public by claiming that the Mexican army had started the war. More important, Lincoln was a leader in drafting a plan to phase out slavery in Washington, D.C.

This plan would set up a referendum, meaning

The flag of Liberia. In the 1820s, the American Colonization Society (ACS) began arranging for free blacks to move to settlements in Africa rather than remain in the United States. In 1847, these settlements became the nation of Liberia. By 1867, more than 13,000 freed slaves had relocated there. The original African-American settlers of Liberia and their descendants are known as Americo-Liberians.

These maps show the location of the District of Columbia (Washington, D.C.). As a federal district, Washington is not part of any state, and so it was not affected by the same laws regarding slavery as the surrounding states. During the Civil War, its location placed it squarely between Maryland, which belonged to the Union, and Virginia, which belonged to the Confederacy.

the people of Washington would vote "yes" or "no" on different plans for freeing slaves. Because women and people of color did not have voting rights, voters were defined as adult white males, and none of the city's 10,000 free blacks would have a say. In any event, Lincoln's plan was not approved by Congress, there was never a referendum in D.C., and slavery continued in the nation's capital until 1862.

Lincoln ran for only one term in Congress and, in 1849, the Lincolns returned to Illinois. There, he quietly resumed his law career. At age 40, Lincoln's career in politics seemed to have fizzled out.

The Lincolns Return to Springfield

Back in Springfield, home life for the Lincolns was not entirely happy. Lincoln spent many days and nights working on out-of-town cases and trials. Despite being moody and depressed, he enjoyed success and celebrity as a lawyer. In the 1840s and 1850s, many people attended court for entertainment. Lincoln's courtroom speeches mixed powerful, clear legal arguments with funny stories.

By 1849, the Lincolns had two sons—Robert, born in 1843, and Edward (Eddie), born in 1846. Early in 1850, Eddie died shortly before his fourth birthday. Understandably, Eddie's death devastated the Lincolns. Abraham vowed to

Abraham Lincoln while a traveling lawyer, photographed in Danville, Illinois.

25

This Lincoln family portrait was painted in 1861. From left: Mary, Willie, Robert, Tad, and Abraham.

spend more time at home and to be a better father. Later that year, Mary gave birth to William (Willie) and, in 1853, they had a fourth son, Thomas (Tad). Lincoln stayed very busy as a father, but he still itched to get back into politics.

During these Springfield years, Lincoln remained a member of the Whig Party, and he helped organize campaigns for local candidates. Meanwhile, the debate over slavery and abolitionism grew louder.

Anti-Slavery Sentiment Continues to Grow

During the 1848 presidential election campaign, neither the Whigs nor the Democrats came out strongly on the issue of slavery. A group of anti-slavery Whigs and Democrats started a new political party. Calling themselves the Free Soil Party, they chose Martin Van Buren as their nominee, and they ran what was basically a one-issue campaign—to oppose extending slavery into the new territories. The Free Soilers had no chance of winning the presidency, but they polled well in the North. This showed that a growing portion of the American people, especially Northerners, agreed with their campaign to stop the spread of slavery.

Lincoln Reconsiders His Opinions on Slavery

The views on slavery that Lincoln adopted from Henry Clay included a condemnation of slavery and beliefs in the humanity of African Americans, a gradual end to slavery, and a program to settle freed slaves in Liberia, Africa. In 1850, Lincoln said, "I can express all my views on the slavery question by quotations from Henry Clay."

When Henry Clay died in 1852, Lincoln began to question his own commitment to Clay's views on slavery. After more than 50 years of emancipationist campaigning, slavery was stronger than ever. The idea of phasing out slavery with the cooperation of slave owners simply had not worked. Lincoln lost confidence in the goal of gradually eliminating slavery, but he also could not support the abolitionist goal of putting an immediate, total, and unconditional end to slavery.

Until the Civil War, much of the conflict over slavery focused on the slave policy in the new territories. In 1820, when Abraham Lincoln was a boy, there was a national clamor over whether Missouri should be admitted to the Union as a free state or as a slave state. Henry Clay forged a compromise. Missouri would be admitted as a slave state, and Maine would enter as a free state. Going forward, any new state admitted from territory north of Missouri's southern border would be a free state. Any new state south of Missouri's southern border could be, but did not have to be, a slave state. With this agreement, passed in 1820 and known as the Missouri Compromise, territories were granted statehood and admitted to the Union in pairs—one slave and one free.

LEGEND
- U.S. Territories
- Free States
- Slave States
- Missouri Compromise Line

Missouri

This map shows the Missouri Compromise line and the resulting distribution of slave and free states by the late 1840s. According to the terms of the original Compromise, Missouri would be admitted into the Union as a slave state, and all territories west of Missouri would become free or slave states, depending on which side of the line they were on. On this map, eventual state boundaries are shown for reference.

The Mexican-American War and the Kansas-Nebraska Act

In 1846, emancipationists feared that this balance between slave and free states was about to be threatened. Any land that the United States gained from the 1846–1848 Mexican-American War (see map on page 23) would not be covered by the Missouri Compromise. The increase of U.S. territory to include lands formerly belonging to Mexico became one more spark that inflamed the nation's passions over the issue of slavery in new states and territories.

If the Mexican-American War threatened the Missouri Compromise, the Kansas-Nebraska Act of 1854 did away with it completely. Sponsored by Illinois senator Stephen Douglas, the bill proclaimed the territories of Kansas and Nebraska, both well north of Missouri's southern border, open to slavery if white settlers voted for it. Both pro- and anti-slavery people from neighboring Missouri and other states and territories rushed to Kansas to sway the vote in their favor. The battle between these two groups went beyond the ballot box to attacks and counterattacks.

Almost overnight, the Kansas-Nebraska Act turned U.S. politics upside down. Belonging to one political party or another was often less important than how individuals stood on slavery, and that often came down to whether people were from the North or the South. In the U.S. Congress, many Northern Whigs turned on Southern Whigs. Many Southern Democrats turned on Northern Democrats.

When Congress created two new territories—Kansas and Nebraska—it sparked a bloody conflict between defenders and opponents of slavery.

In 1856, Charles Sumner, an anti-slavery senator from Massachusetts, was beaten on the floor of the U.S. Senate by Preston S. Brooks, a pro-slavery congressman from South Carolina, The beating came following a speech in which Sumner had criticized the Kansas-Nebraska Act and called for the immediate admission of Kansas into the Union as a free state. Clearly, the issue of slavery was rising to the boiling point throughout the United States in the years leading up to the Civil War.

The Power of the "Peoria Speech"

The Kansas-Nebraska Act disturbed Lincoln and further shook his confidence in Henry Clay's vision of a gradual end to slavery. As he had before, and as he would time and again, Lincoln relied on his talents for self-education. He took to the library for weeks, reading everything he could that the Founding Fathers had written about slavery around the time that the United States had become a nation. He emerged with a 17,000-word speech in his hand. It is the longest speech Lincoln ever delivered, and all three hours of it addressed only one issue—slavery.

The speech was an attack not only on the expansion of slavery, but against "the monstrous injustice of slavery itself." Lincoln said that slavery violated the principles of the Declaration of Independence, which proclaimed that "all men are created equal" and entitled to liberty. He argued that the Founding Fathers never intended slavery to expand to the territories. In language stronger than he had ever used before, Lincoln called for the "ultimate extinction" of slavery.

Lincoln gave this speech in the Illinois city of Peoria in October 1854, then elsewhere in the state. It was published in newspapers in its entirety. It was attacked by pro-slavery readers and cheered by anti-slavery readers. The popularity of his "Peoria speech" encouraged Lincoln to run for the U.S. Senate later in that same year, 1854.

At the time, U.S. senators were not elected by a direct vote of the people. People voted for representatives to their state's legislature, and the legislators voted for the two senators who would represent their state in Washington. Realizing that he didn't have enough votes to win the election, Lincoln threw his support behind another candidate, who went on to win. Though Abe was disappointed, the other Illinois Senate seat came up for election in 1858. Abe started to plan his campaign.

The Lincoln-Douglas Debates

Soon after the Kansas-Nebraska Act passed, many anti-slavery Whigs, Northern Democrats, and anti-slavery leaders from other parties united to form a new political party called the Republicans. Lincoln remained loyal to the Whig Party for as long as he could but, by the time of the 1858 U.S. Senate race in Illinois, he ran as a Republican.

At the 1858 Illinois Republican convention, the delegates made Lincoln their unanimous choice as their party's candidate for the Senate. In his now-famous acceptance speech, he said: "'A house divided against itself cannot stand.' I believe this government cannot endure permanently half slave and half free."

Lincoln's opponent was Stephen A. Douglas, the Illinois Democrat who had sponsored the Kansas-Nebraska Act. At age 45, Douglas was a prominent politician with ambitions to run for president. Lincoln and Douglas clashed in a series of seven three-hour debates spanning nearly two months, August 21 to October 15, 1858. In many ways, the debates were not just a contest between two men vying for a job as U.S. senator—they debated for the soul of America.

The entire nation turned its eyes to the men, to the events, and to the issues. Newspapers from around the nation sent stenographers, runners, and reporters to each of the seven debates. By most accounts, Douglas won the first two or three debates. He called Lincoln

Abraham Lincoln prior to running for the U.S. Senate in 1958.

The Dred Scott Decision

The fight over slavery was fueled by a legal case that made its way to the U.S. Supreme Court in 1857. Dred Scott was a slave who had lived with his master, an army surgeon, in the free state of Illinois and the free territory of Wisconsin. When Scott's master died, Scott filed a lawsuit to win his freedom in the courts. In a decision known as "Dred Scott v. Sanford," the Court ruled that Scott had to be returned to his current owner. In the eyes of the Court, people of African ancestry—slaves as well as those who were free—were not U.S. citizens and therefore could not sue in federal court. The decision also declared that since slaves were property, slave owners had the right to take their "property" into any and all federal territories, slave or free.

The Dred Scott Decision is credited with further hardening anti-slavery feelings in the North in the lead-up to the Civil War. It also provided Abraham Lincoln with a burst of political energy that would result in his election to the presidency of the United States in 1860.

an abolitionist who would give African Americans the right to vote and allow marriage between the races. He accused Lincoln of encouraging mob violence and rebellion. In 1858, even many of the anti-slavery members of the audience found these representations of Lincoln frightening and distasteful. But Lincoln kept insisting that slavery was morally wrong. The Declaration of Independence, said Lincoln, gave all people—white and black alike—the freedoms of "life, liberty, and the pursuit of happiness." Douglas's personal attacks seemed petty by comparison to Lincoln's powerful ideas and use of language.

"Lincoln for President!"

As many as 25,000 people attended the October debates, while a million more followed the drama in newspapers. Although Lincoln lost this election, his reputation as an anti-slavery leader spread throughout the North and the South alike. Republicans now whispered: "Lincoln for president." By 1860, the whispers had given way to banners and cheers.

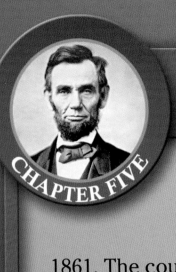
President Lincoln and the Civil War

New Year's Day, 1863. Abraham Lincoln has been president of the United States since March 1861. The country is divided. Eleven of the 33 states have seceded, or left the United States. They have formed the Confederate States of America, and are now at war with the Union. Lincoln sits at a desk in his White House office.

The Emancipation Proclamation, a document that will forever change slavery in the United States, lies on the desk before him. He looks at his secretary of state, William Seward, and declares, "I never, in my life, felt more certain that I was doing right, than I do in signing this paper." He pauses, steadies his hand and, in clear, bold handwriting, puts his name to the document.

Becoming Known

Even before his highly publicized 1858 debates with Stephen Douglas, Abraham Lincoln began to make his name known among members of the new Republican Party. At their 1856 convention, the party nominated, for the first time, a Republican ticket of candidates for president and vice president. They also adopted a party platform, or set of actions they supported and presented to the voters, of admitting Kansas to the Union as a free state and prohibiting slavery in all the territories.

Lincoln's name was placed in nomination for vice president in 1856. Although the delegates did not choose him, the 1856 convention made Lincoln's name familiar to national Republican Party members, and it was clear that many Republicans considered him a potential leader.

Opposite: Following Abraham Lincoln's issuing of the Emancipation Proclamation, many slaves freed by Union troops in the South went on to join the Union military. Shown here: a detail from a sculpture honoring the 54th Massachusetts Volunteer Infantry Regiment. The 54th was one of the first all-African-American Union regiments to fight in the Civil War. Organized in March 1863, the regiment's courage on the battlefield helped convince Congress to grant equal pay to black soldiers and white soldiers. The 54th has been the subject of many works of art and literature and, in 1989, its story was portrayed in the award-winning movie *Glory*. Among the most notable battlefield achievements by the 54th was its July 1863 attack on heavily defended Fort Wagner in South Carolina.

Two years later, in 1858, despite losing the Senate race to Douglas in Illinois, Lincoln's performance at the debates furthered his reputation as a national Republican leader. The delegates at the 1860 Republican convention made him their candidate for president.

The Presidential Election of 1860

The election of 1860 was unusual because four major candidates were running for president. Northern and Southern Democrats split on the issue of slavery. Northern Democrats nominated

This 1860 presidential campaign button features a portrait of Lincoln done as a tintype, which is a photo developed directly onto a sheet of metal.

Stephen Douglas, the senator from Illinois. Meanwhile, Southern Democrats held their own convention and nominated former vice president John Breckinridge. Also, a new party was formed called the Constitutional Union Party. This new party's main issue was to make sure that nothing, especially slavery policies, would threaten to break up the United States. They nominated former congressman John Bell. The Republicans united behind Lincoln.

With four candidates, no one candidate received a majority of the popular vote. In the United States, the president is not directly elected by popular vote. The election is decided by the votes of a group of electors known as the Electoral College. Each state has a certain number of electors based on the state's population. In almost all the states, the candidate who gets more votes than any other candidate in that state, even if it is not the majority of the vote, receives all the Electoral College votes from that state.

Although Abraham Lincoln received only 40 percent of the popular

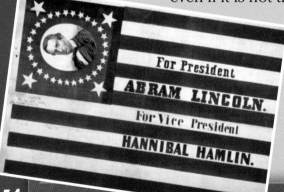

A large cotton banner for Abraham Lincoln and his running mate, Hannibal Hamlin, for president and vice president in 1860. Perhaps for reasons of space, Lincoln is referred to on this banner as "Abram Lincoln."

vote, he won the 1860 presidential election with almost 60 percent of the electoral votes. And so, with only eight years of political experience at the state level and two years as a U.S. congressman, Abraham Lincoln, age 51, became the 16th president of the United States.

This map shows which states were won by the four candidates in the 1860 presidential election. In some states, such as Illinois and Indiana, Lincoln barely won half the popular vote. In others, such as California and Oregon, he received less than half the vote. By winning more than any of the other three candidates, however, he was able to claim all of those states' electoral votes.

Secession and Civil War

In the 1860 presidential election, Lincoln and the Republicans did not wage a fist-shaking, abolitionist campaign. They did call slavery immoral, and the Republican position was that slavery could not exist legally in the territories. They did not argue for the abolition of slavery in states where it already existed. Still, many Southerners viewed Lincoln and other Republicans as a threat to their slave-based way of life. During the four months between election day (November 6, 1860) and the inauguration (March 4, 1861), when Lincoln was officially sworn in as president, seven Southern states declared themselves independent from the United States. These states were South Carolina, Mississippi, Florida, Alabama, Georgia, Louisiana, and Texas.

Leaders from these states met in Montgomery, Alabama, in February 1861 and, between February 4 and 8, they formed the Confederate States of America. In the three months after Lincoln's March 4 inauguration as president of the United States, these seven states were joined by four more states—Virginia, Arkansas, North Carolina, and Tennessee.

The secession of the first seven states posed an immediate challenge to Lincoln's presidency. On April 12, 1861, a little more than a month after Lincoln's inauguration, the situation became even more alarming. The Confederate army surrounded Fort Sumter, a U.S. fort off the coast of South Carolina, and demanded that U.S. forces abandon the fort. When the Union commander refused to abandon Fort Sumter, the Confederate army attacked. Two days later, Union soldiers surrendered the fort. Although there were no soldier casualties on either side, with this battle, the Civil War had begun.

Flags of the Union and the Confederacy.

Jefferson Davis—Lincoln's Counterpart in the Confederacy

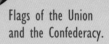

Jefferson Davis was president of the Confederate States of America from 1861–1865. Davis was a former colonel in the U.S. Army, a member of the U.S. House of Representatives, and Secretary of War under U.S. president Franklin Pierce. He was serving in the U.S. Senate when, on January 9, 1861, it was announced that the state he represented, Mississippi, had declared its independence from the United States. On January 21, calling it the "saddest day of my life," he said farewell to his colleagues in the Senate and returned to Mississippi. Only a few weeks later, on February 22, he was chosen as the first and only president of the Confederacy.

General Robert E. Lee, who commanded all Confederate forces by the end of the Civil War in 1865, had been offered a Union army command just before the Civil War began in 1861. Lee felt personal loyalty to the United States and criticized secession as a way of resolving differences between the North and the South. When Virginia seceded, however, Lee knew he could not command an army that would invade his home state, and he therefore resigned from the United States Army on April 20, 1861. Soon after that, he became a general in the Confederate States Army.

The bad news continued. Within a few months of the start of Lincoln's first term, one in three U.S. army officers resigned and enlisted with Confederate armies. Foremost among those whom the Union lost to the Confederacy was the brilliant tactician, or military planner, Robert E. Lee.

Wartime President

Up until his election as president of the United States, Abraham Lincoln's experience as a lawyer and politician had taught him how to deliver a powerful speech, research laws, write legislation, and work within his own party to organize election campaigns. In 1861, however, he found himself in what was, for him, the entirely new position of commander-in-chief during a time of war.

If Lincoln lacked experience, the one ability on which he could rely was his talent for self-education. As he had at other times in his life, Lincoln took to the library, this time to teach himself the military science that would make him a successful wartime president. For all his experience, however, teaching himself such a complex branch of knowledge was an uphill struggle.

In the first few months after the attack on Fort Sumter, the war did not go well for Lincoln or the Union. The Union had more soldiers, more weapons, and more supplies than the Confederates, but these advantages did not translate into the kind of military superiority that one might expect. Throughout most of Lincoln's first term, the rebels were never very far from victory. A large part of the blame for this lay with the shortcomings of many of the Union army generals.

This map shows the alignment of states forming the Union and the Confederacy by the end of the Civil War. The Confederate States are red. The United States are blue. The light blue states are the so-called border states—slave states that remained in the Union. They are, from west to east, Missouri, Kentucky, West Virginia, Maryland, and Delaware. West Virginia broke away from the Confederate state of Virginia and was admitted into the Union in 1863. The gray areas are U.S. territories that had not yet achieved statehood prior to the Civil War.

The Civil War was fought primarily on two theaters, or fronts. Unskilled Union generals on both the eastern and western fronts frustrated Lincoln and hurt the Union cause.

From June 1862 to June 1863, no fewer than five different generals led the Union Army of the Potomac, on the eastern front. On the western front, Lincoln's luck in choosing generals who were decisive and capable leaders was nearly as bad. The possibility grew that the military superiority of the rebel forces might be enough to force the Union to sign a treaty recognizing the Confederate States as an independent nation. By the summer of 1862, Lincoln knew something had to be done.

To Save the Union

From the start of the war in April 1861, the Confederates were fighting primarily to preserve the institution of slavery. Lincoln's goal at the time was primarily to preserve the Union. In addition to the 11 Southern states that seceded following Lincoln's election, four other states were slave states. These four states—Maryland, Delaware, Kentucky, and Missouri, were collectively known as the border states. Unlike the 11 other slave states, the border states stayed in the Union. Lincoln understood the military importance of keeping these states in the Union, and he worried that some or all might leave the Union to join the Confederacy.

To keep the loyalty of these border states, Lincoln assured them that the purpose of the war was to preserve the Union, not to end slavery. When, in May 1861, hundreds of slaves escaped from border states and sought refuge with the Union army, Lincoln ordered his generals to return the fugitive slaves to their owners. Furthermore, in August 1861, Union General John C. Frémont freed the slaves of Confederate sympathizers in Missouri, Lincoln overturned the order. Lincoln hoped these loyal border states would eventually end slavery voluntarily.

A year later, in August 1862, President Lincoln wrote a letter published in a popular newspaper, declaring:

> *If I could save the Union without freeing any slave I would do it, and if I could save it by freeing all the slaves I would do it; and if I could save it by freeing some and leaving others alone I would also do that.*

The Emancipation Proclamation

Public statements such as this made many Northerners believe that reuniting the United States, not ending slavery, was Lincoln's main goal. This was not the entire story, however. Only a few of Lincoln's closest advisers knew that even as he was writing his "save the Union" letter, he was already working on a plan that would greatly alter the goal of the war and the future of slavery in America.

The seeds for these changes lay in the document called the Emancipation Proclamation. With the Proclamation, Lincoln and the Union took steps that had never been taken before the Civil War. These steps included allowing the federal government to interfere with the slavery laws of individual states.

Lincoln wrote an early draft of the Emancipation Proclamation in July 1862. At the time, some Northerners had grown weary of the war. Many dozens of battles were waged in the first half of 1862, and the tolls of dead and wounded were high. Some Democrats, known as "Peace Democrats," called on Lincoln to meet with the Confederates and to accept their policies on slavery. While most Republicans supported Lincoln's handling of the war, some urged him to conduct the war even more aggressively and to make the end of slavery the central purpose of the war. These debates were conducted in Congress, in the newspapers, and among the citizens and the families of soldiers.

In April 1862, led by a group of aggressive anti-slavery senators and congressmen known as "Radical Republicans," Congress had passed a bill ending slavery in Washington, D.C., and Lincoln signed it into law. The bill was similar to one he had unsuccessfully proposed in 1848, when he was a congressman from Illinois. Now, in 1862, the law gave Lincoln a powerful weapon. It was, at the time, the only law in the nation that actually outlawed slavery, and it helped excite anti-slavery feelings among Northern lawmakers and citizens alike. In July 1862, Congress passed another bill, supported by Lincoln, that banned slavery in all federal territory, not just in Washington, D.C.

What Lincoln was about to propose in his Emancipation Proclamation went even farther than these bills, which did not apply to the states themselves. The Proclamation declared that "all persons held as slaves within any State or designated part of a State... in rebelliion against the United States, shall be... forever free."

Because Lincoln did not recognize the Confederacy as an independent nation, granting freedom to all slaves in states "in rebellion against the United States" referred specifically to the Confederate States.

Presidential War Powers

Lincoln knew that the U.S. Constitution did not give the federal government the power to simply end slavery in any state where it already existed. To resolve this problem, Lincoln invoked, or turned to, his rights as commander-in-chief of the military. As head of the armed forces, the president is allowed to take

A Confederate 100-dollar bill. The illustration in the center shows slaves working in a cotton field.

certain actions when the security of the country is threatened. These actions are called "war powers." In fact, Lincoln had already used these powers in 1861. During a period of anti-Union rioting in Maryland, Lincoln commanded the army to arrest anyone suspected of disloyalty.

This photograph shows a group of fugitive slaves joining U.S. troops behind Union lines. During the Civil War, many escaped slaves fled to the Union army, where they were called "contraband." This term was used to give the Union the authority to keep the slaves as "property" seized during the war, rather than return them to their owners in the South. Once the Emancipation Proclamation was issued in 1863, the Union had, by presidential decree, the right to declare the slaves free. At that point, many of them joined the fight against the Confederacy.

Lincoln also examined all the ways slavery helped the Confederate cause, and hurt the Union, on the battlefield. The rebel army brought slaves to the battlefields. The slaves dug trenches, cooked for the soldiers, and attended to their wounds and illnesses. Slaves in service to the Confederate army freed Confederate soldiers to engage in combat with Union soldiers. Lincoln came to the conclusion that slaves forced into serving the Confederate cause would lead to more Confederate victories, and more Union soldier injuries and deaths.

If, as a "necessary war measure," Lincoln declared slavery abolished, Union soldiers would be ordered to free any slaves they encountered as they pushed into Confederate territory. Knowing that Union troops would accept them, other Southern slaves might be encouraged to escape and even join the Union forces. Therefore, the tide of the war could swing to the Union. It could be argued, then, that emancipation was necessary to a Union victory, and it was covered by the presidential war powers.

President Abraham Lincoln meets with General George B. McClellan at the battlefield at Antietam, Maryland. Antietam was the victory Lincoln needed to set the stage for making the preliminary Emancipation Proclamation public in September 1862.

Making the Proclamation Public

The Emancipation Proclamation was to go into effect on January 1, 1863. When Lincoln discussed the first draft of the Proclamation with his cabinet on July 22, 1862, they supported him. Secretary of State William Seward recommended, however, that Lincoln wait for a decisive Union army victory before making the Proclamation public. Following his advice, Lincoln kept the Proclamation under wraps while waiting for the decisive Union win.

That victory came on September 17, 1862, when Union and Confederate armies clashed at Antietam, Maryland. Five thousand soldiers died that day, and the Confederate army retreated to Virginia. Five days later, on September 22, the U.S. government published the preliminary Emancipation Proclamation.

In the North, free blacks, abolitionists, and their supporters rejoiced. Spontaneous celebrations spilled out onto the streets. A large crowd of supporters sang songs outside the White House. But Peace Democrats in the North did not share this joy. Through speeches, newspaper articles, and posters, they issued dire, racist warnings that freed slaves might attack white women and children and take away jobs from white men.

This print celebrating the Emancipation Proclamation was created around the time that Lincoln signed the Proclamation in 1863. It shows two slaves embracing a U.S. flag. Between them stands *Columbia*, the female symbol for the United States.

In the South, the preliminary Proclamation put Confederate leaders on notice that they had 100 days to cease their rebellion or lose their right to own slaves. If, however, they rejoined the Union, they would be allowed to keep their slaves, at least for the time being. When the Proclamation went into effect on January 1, 1863, no Southern states had rejoined the Union.

African-American Union Soldiers

The final version of the Proclamation, revised just before Lincoln signed it on January 1, 1863, permitted the recruitment of African Americans into the military. Black soldiers had already been serving since July 1862, but the government paid them less than white soldiers and most often assigned them the non-combat chores of digging ditches or preparing meals. Now, African-American soldiers would be armed, fighting, and dying for the Union cause. Black soldiers in the Union army would have to wait until June 1864, however, before Congress granted them equal pay.

Though led in battle by white officers, black soldiers distinguished themselves in several fierce battles. By the time the war ended, 200,000 African Americans had served in the Union military.

The Emancipation Proclamation did not free the 500,000 slaves in the

"If the people over the river had behaved themselves, I could not have done what I have; but they did not, and I was compelled to do these things."

— Abraham Lincoln on his freeing of the slaves, as he pointed toward Virginia, which was in the Confederacy. He said this to Sojourner Truth (above), the famed activist, reformer, and former slave, shown here in a painting with Lincoln during her visit with him in Washington, D.C., in 1864.

A rare photo of black and white soldiers, here a group of teenagers, serving together in the Union army.

border states of Maryland, Missouri, Delaware, and Kentucky, which were still part of the Union. Nor did it apply to Tennessee, which was largely occupied by the Union by then. It also did not apply to certain counties in Virginia, including those that were about to become the U.S. state of West Virginia. Emancipation in some of those states would come by individual state actions. In others, it would come with the approval, in December 1865, of the Thirteenth Amendment to the U.S. Constitution. The Thirteenth Amendment made slavery illegal everywhere in the United States.

Even without these immediate results in the border region, the Proclamation was a stunning triumph for the anti-slavery cause. Combining military determination with the moral goal of freeing slaves, the Union's purpose in the war became newly focused. If the Union won, the states would be reunited as a new country—a country where slavery would be a thing of the past. The Proclamation also rallied the Confederates, who were equally determined to defend their slave-based way of life.

African-American Union soldiers fighting at an abandoned farmhouse in Virginia in 1864.

Gettysburg

In 1863, several battles of historic importance were fought. In early May, General Lee scored perhaps his greatest military victory, driving Union troops out of Virginia and back into Pennsylvania. As with all major Civil War battles, casualties and human suffering were staggering on both sides.

In a war filled with horrific battles, possibly the most horrific battle of the Civil War was the Battle of Gettysburg in the Union state of Pennsylvania. There, 170,000 soldiers fought for three days, from July 1–3, 1863. By the end, Union and Confederate casualties combined totaled 7,000 dead, 34,000 seriously wounded, and 11,000 missing. When Confederate troops invaded Pennsylvania, 80,000 Union troops met them. A Confederate victory might have forced Lincoln to negotiate a peace and recognize the Confederate States of America as a separate, slave-based country. Even before Gettysburg, some Union Democratic leaders and war-weary citizens in the North called on Lincoln to negotiate with the Confederacy to end the war.

General Ulysses S. Grant, as photographed at his military headquarters in Cold Harbor, Virginia, in 1864. His leadership and success on the battlefield led President Lincoln to make him commanding general of all Union armies. In that position, Grant helped turn the tide of war toward the Union.

The Confederates did not win the Battle of Gettysburg, however. With 28,000 Confederate soldiers dead or wounded, Lee retreated to Virginia. On the western front, Union forces commanded by General Ulysses S. Grant captured the key position of Vicksburg, Mississippi. This gave the Union navy control of the entire Mississippi River.

To both sides, this seemed to be the turning point of the war. After these Union victories, Confederate President Jefferson Davis sent Vice President Alexander H. Stephens to negotiate a peace. Lincoln, too, saw these battles as a turning point that could lead to a Union victory. He wanted nothing less than unconditional surrender, meaning only Lincoln and the Union could make the terms of surrender. The Confederacy would have no say, and Lincoln refused to meet with Stephens.

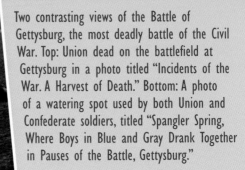

Two contrasting views of the Battle of Gettysburg, the most deadly battle of the Civil War. Top: Union dead on the battlefield at Gettysburg in a photo titled "Incidents of the War. A Harvest of Death." Bottom: A photo of a watering spot used by both Union and Confederate soldiers, titled "Spangler Spring, Where Boys in Blue and Gray Drank Together in Pauses of the Battle, Gettysburg."

The war continued. Before the end of 1863, Grant led his Union troops to major battle victories in Tennessee and Georgia. Such losses took a heavy toll on the morale and the military of the Confederates.

The Gettysburg Address and the Purpose of the War

On November 19, 1863, 15,000 people gathered near the site of the Battle of Gettysburg for ceremonies dedicating the battlefield, where so many had died, as a Soldiers' National Cemetery. President Lincoln delivered a brief but very important speech, known as the Gettysburg Address.

In 273 powerful and eloquent words, the Gettysburg Address made it clear that Lincoln saw emancipation—not just reunification—as a central purpose of the war. Lincoln had long felt that the Declaration of Independence contained language that argued against the institution of slavery. So it was important that, in his own Gettysburg Address, he echoed the Founding Fathers' words that "all men are created equal," and focused on "Liberty" and "a new birth of freedom."

Reaction to the speech was generally quite positive, although few who heard it may have understood how history would come to cherish it for its message and its carefully crafted style in phrases such as these:

> *Four score and seven years ago our fathers brought forth on this continent, a new nation, conceived in Liberty, and dedicated to the proposition that all men are created equal... [W]e here highly resolve that these dead shall not have died in vain—that this nation, under God, shall have a new birth of freedom—and that government of the people, by the people, for the people, shall not perish from the earth.*

Among newspapers and politicians, the reactions were mostly along party lines. Republicans praised the speech, and Northern Democrats and Democratic-leaning newspapers criticized the speech for emphasizing freedom over the preservation of the Union.

As 1864 rolled around, so did the presidential election campaigns. Lincoln knew that if he did not win re-election, the causes of saving the Union and abolishing slavery would be lost. He knew, too, that his chances for re-election hinged on winning the war.

One of the few known photographs of Abraham Lincoln (circled) taken on the day of his Gettysburg Address. He is shown shortly after his arrival, and about three hours before his speech. The president, when later complimented on his speech, replied that he was simply glad it hadn't been a "total failure."

CHAPTER SIX

The Thirteenth Amendment and Lincoln's Legacy

For the 1864 presidential election, the Democrats nominated George B. McClellan, one of Lincoln's former generals. McClellan and the Democrats promised to repeal, or abolish, the Emancipation Proclamation and to negotiate peace with the Confederacy. Since 1861, nearly one in every ten young men of service age died in the war, with countless others physically and psychologically scarred by battle. To many, the Democrats' platform seemed reasonable, especially if there was no Union victory in sight.

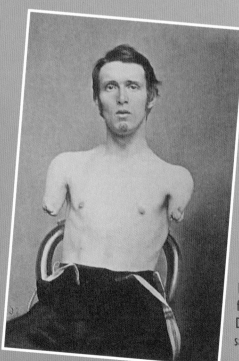

Everyone knew someone who had died in the Civil War, parents who lost sons, soldiers who returned home missing a leg or an arm, and others who returned physically whole, but traumatized by the killing and the bloodshed. This Union soldier, 19-year-old Alfred A. Stratton, was hit by cannon fire. Following his recovery from his amputation, he had photos of himself made into cards he could sell to help him earn a living. He went on to become a husband, a father, and a pastor at churches in New York and Washington, D.C. He died at the age of 29 of a condition that doctors said was related to his having been wounded in the war.

Lincoln Is Nominated for Re-election

Despite some grumbling about replacing him as their presidential candidate, the Republicans nominated Lincoln to run for re-election in 1864. At the Republican national convention in June 1864, Lincoln and the Republicans took two bold stands. They promised to continue waging an aggressive war until the Confederacy surrendered unconditionally. They also promised to abolish slavery throughout the United States.

Two months before the Republican convention in June, Congress had considered an amendment, or addition, to the U.S. Constitution to abolish slavery. That addition, the Thirteenth Amendment to the Constitution, is simple, and it reads as follows:

> "*Section 1.* Neither slavery nor involuntary servitude, except as a punishment for crime whereof the party shall have been duly convicted, shall exist within the United States, or any place subject to their jurisdiction.
>
> *Section 2.* Congress shall have power to enforce this article by appropriate legislation."

The Senate passed the Thirteenth Amendment in April 1864, but in two votes, the House of Representatives failed to pass it. It became clear that passing the bill in the House might require Lincoln to use his power as a re-elected president. If Lincoln did not win re-election in November, the Thirteenth Amendment's chances for success would be doubtful.

The War, and Lincoln's Presidency, Continue

Before the November 1864 election, General Ulysses S. Grant, now commander of all Union forces, and Confederate General Robert E. Lee clashed in a series of bloody battles. In the Battle of Cold Harbor,

Peace Democrats tried to panic Northern voters by claiming that Republicans promoted dating and marriage between blacks and whites, behavior they called "miscegenation." They published false accounts and posters like this, which shows Republicans and black southern belles dancing up a storm at "The Miscegenation Ball."

Virginia, Confederate soldiers killed or seriously wounded 7,000 Union soldiers in the first hour alone. The battle lasted two weeks in June, and the Confederates held their ground. This news was not good for Lincoln and his chances for re-election.

With Grant in the east, General William Tecumseh Sherman stepped up to lead the Union army on the western front. On July 22, 1864, Sherman's army drove the Confederate army out of Atlanta, which was the largest and most important city in Georgia, ordered the city's residents to leave, then burned most of the buildings to the ground.

With news of Sherman's success, citizens and newspapers believed victory was in sight, and Lincoln's chances for re-election improved. In the November election, Lincoln won with 55 percent of the popular vote, and an even larger majority of the electoral vote.

Lincoln Lobbies for the Thirteenth Amendment

All the while, Lincoln and his staff were wheeling and dealing to get the Thirteenth Amendment, which would outlaw slavery, passed in the House of Representatives. After the election, Lincoln sought out "lame duck" congressmen who had lost in November but would still be in

Lincoln in February 1860, the year of his election to the presidency.

Personal Life and Tragedy in the Lincoln White House

As president, Lincoln's appearance aged quickly. The war took its toll on him, and his personal life offered little comfort.

What is considered the last-known photograph of Lincoln, taken in March 1865, about a month before his death.

In 1861, the Lincoln family arrived at the White House with three sons. Eighteen-year-old Robert attended Harvard, and for most of his father's presidency, he stayed in Massachusetts. Meanwhile, the White House became home and playground to ten-year-old Willie and eight-year-old Tad.

The refreshing joy brought to the White House by the sight of two young and mischievous boys soon turned to anguish. In February 1862, Willie became ill and died. He was 11. Devastated, Mary Lincoln isolated herself and grieved for two years.

Faced with making decisions that affected the lives and deaths of young American soldiers, Lincoln could not rely on Mary for moments of solace and comfort. Instead, he shared his most affectionate moments with

Tad and his father were often seen together, telling stories, looking at pictures, and reading books. In this photograph, taken in 1864, the two are shown looking through a photo album.

his youngest son, Tad. Spoiled and a little wild, Tad had the complete run of the White House. Tad died of tuberculosis in 1871. Robert Lincoln, who lived until 1926, when he died at the age of 82, was the only Lincoln child to live past the age of 18.

Willie (center) and Tad (right) Lincoln, with their cousin Lockwood Todd, in 1861.

A photo of Robert Todd Lincoln, probably taken sometime around 1922.

office until January. Lincoln felt that those who had been against the amendment might now be persuaded to change their vote. He offered many of them jobs as ambassadors, judges, tax agents—whatever it took. More than a dozen of these congressmen changed their vote. On January 31, 1865, five weeks before Lincoln's second inauguration, the House passed the Thirteenth Amendment, thereby abolishing slavery.

Spontaneous celebrations spilled into the streets of Washington, D.C., and many other Northern cities. The bill now had to be ratified, or approved, by three-quarters of the states. Illinois ratified it immediately. It would be almost a year before the remaining three-quarters of the states ratified the bill but, that night, Lincoln was joyful. He began his political career vaguely opposed to slavery. Now, 32 years later, he fulfilled the vision of the abolitionists. In some corners in the South, however, men and women of a different mind gathered to plot their next move.

War's End at Last!

In 1864, after driving Confederate troops from Atlanta, General Sherman led his Union troops to Savannah, also in Georgia, in a military campaign known as "Sherman's March to the Sea." Along the way, his troops destroyed Confederate military and industrial targets, destroying the

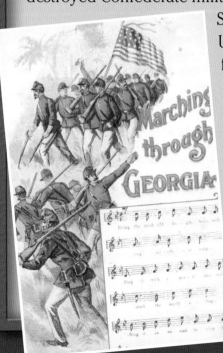

South's ability to fight the war. By early 1865, Union forces increasingly outnumbered rebel forces with every battle.

On March 4, 1865, the ceremony and celebrations of Lincoln's second inauguration took place. Anticipating that an end to the Civil War was near, Lincoln reached out to friend and foe alike in his second inaugural address. Though the

This postcard, created around 1902, shows Union soldiers marching to the song "Marching through Georgia." The song, written in 1865 after the campaign known as "Sherman's March to the Sea," became a standard worldwide, especially during times of war.

This grainy image is the only known photo of President Lincoln delivering his second inaugural address. He may be spotted (circled), holding papers in his hand and standing in the center, and in the enlarged view (inset).

Gettysburg Address is Lincoln's best-known speech, many historians consider this brief, six-minute speech his best. In it, he anticipated, with the coming Union victory, the end to slavery. But he did not brag of that victory. Rather, he asked the following of the nation in these powerful and famous words:

> "With malice toward none; with charity for all… let us strive on to finish the work we are in; to bind up the nation's wounds; to care for him who shall have borne the battle, and for his widow, and his orphan—to do all which may achieve and cherish a just and a lasting peace, among ourselves, and with all nations."

The end of the war came soon after. By April 1865, Lee's army, camped in Richmond, Virginia, was diminished, dispirited, and exhausted. Grant attacked. Lee retreated. Ironically, the first company of Union troops to occupy the Confederate capital was made up of black soldiers. Unable to dodge the pursuit of Grant's army, Lee surrendered a few days later, on April 9, 1865.

Triumph and a Tragic Assassination

Before the end of the war, Lincoln had already begun discussions about how to give African Americans citizenship and the right to vote. The North celebrated victory, and there were undoubtedly many in the South who were glad to be done with the fighting and death. Not everyone

A portrait photo of John Wilkes Booth, taken in 1865, shortly before he assassinated Abraham Lincoln.

could accept the war's outcome, however. Among these was a small band of Southern loyalists led by a well-known actor, John Wilkes Booth. They hatched a plan to throw the United States government into chaos so the Confederate states could reorganize their rebellion. Their plot was hastily put together just five days after the surrender. Booth assigned two men to kill Secretary of State William Seward. A third man was to kill Lincoln's new vice president, Andrew Johnson. Booth himself would kill the President.

Although Seward and several of his family were badly wounded, neither he nor Vice President Johnson were killed. Johnson escaped harm altogether when his assassin thought better of the plan and did not go through with it. Only Booth succeeded in his task of terror.

Booth's plan was to shoot President Lincoln the night of Friday, April 14, 1865. He knew the president, Mrs. Lincoln, and guests would attend a play at Ford's Theatre in Washington. The play was a comedy, *Our American Cousin*. When the big "punch line" of the play came, the audience laughed loudly, as Booth knew they would. At that moment, he stepped into the presidential box seats and, with a handgun, shot Lincoln point blank behind the ear. The President slumped forward, and Booth made his escape.

Lincoln never regained consciousness. He was pronounced dead the next morning.

Booth was hunted down, shot, and killed

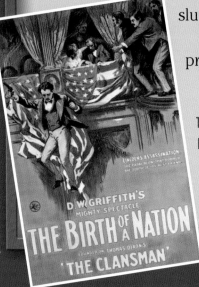

The assassination of President Lincoln and escape by John Wilkes Booth as portrayed on a theatrical poster for the 1915 silent film *The Birth of a Nation*. The D. W. Griffith movie is considered a classic for its technical and artistic techniques. It was strongly criticized, however, and even banned in many cities, for its hateful portrayals of African Americans and glorifying of the racist Ku Klux Klan after the Civil War.

The execution of the four Lincoln conspirators condemned to die by hanging, at Fort McNair, in Washington, D.C., on July 7, 1865.

as he tried to elude arrest. Eight of his co-conspirators were caught, tried by a military tribunal, and convicted. Sentences ranged from six years in prison, to life sentences, to death by hanging. The federal government purchased the Ford Theatre and used it first as an office building, then as a warehouse. In 1968, the building was restored to its 1865 condition and reopened as a museum and a working theater. There is even a presidential box. It is always empty.

After Lincoln

When Lincoln died, Vice President Andrew Johnson was sworn in as president, as dictated by the Constitution. Johnson did not champion equal rights for African Americans under the law as much as Lincoln.

Congress went on to pass the historically momentous Fourteenth Amendment to the U.S. Constitution in 1866 and the Fifteenth Amendment in 1869. The Fourteenth guaranteed the rights of citizenship to all Americans regardless of race, and the Fifteenth assured the right to vote to all American males regardless of race. By 1870, both amendments were ratified by the states.

Reaction was swift from Southern politicians who clung to racist ideas regarding the inferiority of African Americans. Even before the ratification

Vice President Andrew Johnson became the 17th U.S. president when Abraham Lincoln was assassinated. Johnson was a Southern Democrat who firmly supported the Union during the Civil War. But, as president, he often clashed with the Republican-led Congress.

of the Fourteenth and Fifteenth amendments, they began to pass local and state laws, known as "Black Codes," that denied African Americans certain rights such as getting an education or working anywhere except on a farm.

By the 1890s, Southern racists had torn large holes in Lincoln's legacy of emancipation and equality under the law. Although the Confederacy lost, most former Confederate states passed laws such as literacy tests and poll taxes that prevented blacks from voting. They also enforced unwritten practices that barred blacks from mixing with whites, or exercising other privileges of citizenship. African Americans who violated these rules were subject to harassment, mob violence, and sometimes cruel death. As the 1900s, the lasting effects of Lincoln's legacy, and of civil rights for African Americans, were uncertain.

America, Race, and Lincoln's Legacy

In the summer of 1908, an ugly race riot took place in Lincoln's hometown of Springfield, Illinois. The following year, 1909, marked the 100-year anniversary of Lincoln's birth. Celebrations took place throughout the United States. All but one were racially segregated. In 1922, at the dedication ceremonies for the Lincoln Memorial in

Lincoln the Icon

Today, Lincoln's image is one of the most recognized in the world. His face has been on the penny since 1909 and on the five-dollar bill since 1914. Except for George Washington, Lincoln appears on more U.S. stamps than all the rest of the presidents combined, plus stamps from Cuba, Ghana, and dozens of other countries.

Lincoln was the tallest president, the first U.S. president assassinated, and the first president to sport a beard. Lincoln has been portrayed as a character in dozens of movies, from D. W. Griffith's *Abraham Lincoln* (1930) to Steven Spielberg's award-winning *Lincoln* (2012).

South Dakota's magnificent Mount Rushmore National Memorial, where Abraham Lincoln's face rises 60 feet (18 meters) tall. Also carved into the mountain are (from left) the faces of presidents George Washington, Thomas Jefferson, and Theodore Roosevelt.

Washington, D.C., African-American attendees sat in the "colored section." These events and others seemed to disgrace the legacy of a man who risked the unity and possibly the existence of the United States to destroy slavery and to renew the call he heard in the Declaration of Independence for freedom and equality for all.

Yet Lincoln's legacy can be felt at moments of significant achievement in civil rights history, too. In 1939, Marian Anderson, a famous African-American singer, was not allowed to give a concert in Constitution Hall in Washington, D.C., because she was black. She sang instead from the steps of the Lincoln Memorial, before an integrated audience of 75,000.

From those same steps in 1963, civil rights leader Martin Luther King Jr. delivered a moving, historic speech before 200,000 people, black and white. Known as the "I Have a Dream" speech, King's words honored Lincoln by calling the Emancipation Proclamation a "beacon of hope to millions of negro slaves."

As a man and a politician, Abraham Lincoln had his share of flaws. He battled depression. He never felt comfortable in the company of women. For most of his life, he believed that black Americans and white Americans could not live together in harmony, and he supported the

Six million people each year visit the Lincoln Memorial in Washington, D.C. A close look at the back of a penny will reveal the statue of Lincoln sitting inside the building!

idea of convincing free blacks and freed slaves to move to colonies outside the United States.

Nonetheless, most historians recognize Lincoln as a man who did not fail because of his flaws, but who triumphed in spite of them. They recognize Lincoln as a man who raised himself from a dirt-floor cabin to the White House, who guided the United States through perhaps the most dangerous years of its history, and who led the country and its citizens to the abolition of slavery.

Today, 150 years after his death, Abraham Lincoln remains, more than ever, an inspirational hero to world leaders and everyday citizens alike.

A Dramatic, Living, Lincoln Legacy

The election of Barack Obama as 44th president of the United States is one of the most dramatic legacies of Abraham Lincoln, the nation's 16th president. First elected to the presidency in 2008 and re-elected in 2012, Obama found in Lincoln a personal hero—a figure he studied and admired throughout his own political career. In 2009, as he was about to take the oath of office as the first African-American president of the United States, Obama placed his left hand on a red-velvet-colored Bible. It was the same one used by Abraham Lincoln at his inauguration in 1861.

President Barack Obama takes the oath of office at his second inauguration in January 2013. To his right stand First Lady Michelle Obama and their daughters, Malia and Sasha. Supreme Court Chief Justice John Roberts is administering the oath. The first lady is holding two Bibles. The lower one belonged to civil rights leader Martin Luther King Jr. The upper one (also shown above) is the Bible used by Abraham Lincoln for his oath of office in 1861.

1809 Abraham Lincoln is born February 12 in a one-room log cabin in Kentucky.

1816 Family moves to Indiana.

1818 Nancy Hanks Lincoln (Lincoln's mother) dies of milk sickness.

1819 Lincoln's father, Thomas Lincoln, marries Sarah Bush Johnston.

1820 Missouri Compromise passes; divides U.S. territories between slave and free, admits Missouri as slave and Maine as free state. There are 12 slave and 12 free states.

1828 Older sister Sarah dies.

1830 Family moves to Illinois.

1831 Leaves family home to live in New Salem, Illinois; works as clerk in village store.

1832 Black Hawk War breaks out; enlists in Illinois Militia. Runs for Illinois state legislature and loses badly.

1834–1842 Elected to Illinois state legislature four times, serving a total of eight years.

1836 Passes bar exam, starts practicing law.

1837 Moves to Springfield, Illinois.

1842 Marries Mary Todd.

1843–1853 Lincolns have four sons: Robert Todd (1843–1926); Edward Baker (1846–1850); William Wallace (1850–1862); and Thomas (Tad) Lincoln (1853–1871).

1846 Elected to U.S. House of Representatives and family moves to Washington, D.C.; serves one term (1846–1848).

1849 Lincolns move back to Springfield. Lincoln resumes career as traveling attorney.

1850 Son Eddie dies at age three.

1854 Kansas-Nebraska Act passes, overturning Missouri Compromise and reviving debate on slave vs. free states.

1857 U.S. Supreme Court's Dred Scott Decision declares that African Americans do not have the right to sue in courts.

1858 Runs for U.S. Senate against Stephen Douglas; engages in series of debates that draw national attention. Douglas elected.

1860 Nominated by Republican Party as candidate for U.S. presidency; is elected 16th president. South Carolina secedes from Union shortly after election; followed within two months by Mississippi, Florida, Alabama, Georgia, Louisiana, and Texas.

1861 February 4–8: Seven seceded states form Confederate States of America. **February 22:** Jefferson Davis chosen as president of Confederacy. **March 4:** Lincoln inaugurated as U.S. president; within three months four more states—Virginia, Arkansas, North Carolina, and Tennessee—join Confederacy. **April 12:** Confederate artillery opens fire on Fort Sumter in Charleston Harbor, South Carolina; the Civil War begins. **July 21:** Union suffers defeat at Bull Run in northern Virginia; Lincoln realizes war will be a long one.

1862 February: Son Willie dies at age 11, probably from typhoid. **April 16:** Lincoln signs act abolishing slavery in Washington, D.C. **June 19:** Approves law prohibiting slavery in U.S. territories. **July 22:** Presents draft of Emancipation Proclamation to cabinet. **September 17:** Battle of Antietam in Maryland; by nightfall, 26,000 men are dead, wounded, or missing. **September 22:** Issues preliminary Emancipation Proclamation.

1863 January 1: Issues final Emancipation Proclamation, freeing all slaves in states in rebellion against Union. **January 29:** General Ulysses S. Grant placed in command of Army of the West. **May 1–4:** Confederate victory in Battle of Chancellorsville, Virginia. **July 3:** Confederate defeat in Battle of Gettysburg marks turning point of war. **July 4:** Vicksburg, the last Confederate stronghold on the Mississippi, is captured by Grant. **August 10:** Lincoln meets with abolitionist Frederick Douglass, who pushes for full equality for African-American Union soldiers. **November 19:** Delivers Gettysburg Address.

1864 March 12: Appoints Grant commander of all Union armies. **September 2:** Army of the West commander General William Tecumseh Sherman captures Confederate stronghold of Atlanta. **November 8:** Lincoln re-elected president. **December 20:** Union soldiers, in "Sherman's March to the Sea," reach Savannah, leaving path of destruction 60 miles (96.5 km) wide all the way from Atlanta.

1865 March 4: Inauguration in Washington, D.C.; Lincoln delivers Second Inaugural Address. **April 9:** Confederate General Robert E. Lee surrenders his army to Grant at Appomattox Courthouse, Virginia; Civil War all but over. **April 14:** Lincoln and Mary attend play at Ford's Theatre; during third act, John Wilkes Booth shoots president in the head; Lincoln never regains consciousness. **April 15:** Lincoln dies at 7:22 A.M. **December 6:** Thirteenth Amendment to U.S. Constitution, passed by Congress on January 31, 1865, is finally ratified. Slavery is abolished.

abolitionist A person dedicated to ending, or abolishing, the practice of slavery, usually immediately.

amendment A change made to the original U.S. Constitution. The Thirteenth Amendment abolished slavery.

bar exam A test to see whether a person is qualified to practice law.

cabinet An official group of appointed advisers who counsel the president.

casualty A person killed or injured; in the military, a person who can no longer fight due to death, injury, sickness, capture, or unknown whereabouts. There were more than 1,000,000 casualties in the Civil War.

co-conspirator A partner to a plan or plot, usually one that is harmful or unlawful.

colonization Sending groups of settlers to a place and establishing control over that place.

confederate Joined in a group or alliance, often formally, as by a treaty.

contraband Goods seized from an enemy or kept from being delivered to an enemy during time of war. In the Civil War, "contraband" refers to Confederate-owned slaves who escaped or were transported across Union lines and sought refuge in Union camps. Many of these slaves enlisted in African-American regiments of the Union military, known as United States Colored Troops (USCT).

depression A period of sadness, dejection, and hopelessness.

Electoral College A body of people representing states who formally cast votes for the election of the president and vice president. Each state has a certain number of these people, called electors, and usually the winner of each state's popular vote receives all of that states electoral votes.

emancipationist A person supporting a gradual end to slavery, sometimes with compensation to former slave owners for their loss of "property."

free blacks The term used to describe African Americans who were not slaves prior to the abolition of slavery.

general store A rural or small-town store that sells a variety of items such as clothing, hardware, and canned goods. In some areas, especially in the 1800s, it was also a place to get news and share information.

inauguration A ceremony that celebrates the start of an elected official's term.

infrastructure Physical structures and facilities that benefit a city, state, or country, such as buildings, railroads, streets, schools, and power sources.

lame duck An incumbent, or current, holder of a political position who lost the election but is still in office until the election winner takes his or her place.

legislature The branch of government that has the power to make laws; a group of people elected or chosen for that purpose.

malnourished Suffering from the effects of a lack of food or of the right kinds of food that provide proper nutrition.

militia Military troops raised from the local population to support regular troops.

miscegenation Intermarriage between races. Pro-slavery groups tried to create fear by accusing anti-slavery politicians of

promoting intermarriage between freed African-American slaves and whites.

moral Good or honest, having to do with what is right, not wrong.

plantation In reference to the United States before 1865, a large farm in the South worked by African-American slaves.

preliminary Early, opening, or introductory; coming before a final version.

race A classification of humans, usually by physical features.

radical Favoring extreme or very unusual changes.

ramshackle On the verge of falling apart.

ratify To give official approval. Three-fourths, or 75 percent, of all state legislatures must ratify a constitutional amendment before it takes effect.

runner A messenger.

secession The withdrawal, or breaking away, from a group or organization. The secession of 11 states from the United States led to the Civil War.

sermon A speech that offers inspiration or advice, such as one that might be delivered by a minister in a church.

state auditor A person appointed to keep track of a state's financial records.

stenographer A person who uses shorthand to write down what another person says.

suffrage The right to vote.

unanimous In complete agreement (of two or more people).

Further Information

Books

Aronson, Billy. *Abraham Lincoln* (Presidents and Their Times). Benchmark Books, 2009.

Catton, Bruce. *American Heritage Picture History of the Civil War*. Gramercy Press, 1994.

Down, Susan Brophy. *Theodore Weld: Architect of Abolitionism* (Voices for Freedom: Abolitionist Heroes). Crabtree, 2013.

Elliot, Henry. *Frederick Douglass: From Slavery to Statesman* (Voices for Freedom: Abolitionist Heroes). Crabtree, 2010.

Hamilton, Virginia. *Many Thousand Gone: African Americans from Slavery to Freedom*. Knopf Books for Young Readers, 2002.

Judson, Karen. *Abraham Lincoln: "This Nation Shall Have a New Birth of Freedom"* (Americans: The Spirit of a Nation). Enslow, 2008.

Rivera, Sheila. *Abraham Lincoln: A Life of Respect* (Pull Ahead Books). Lerner Books, 2006.

Stanchak, John. *Civil War* (DK Eyewitness Books). DK Publishing, Inc., 2000.

Websites

www.abrahamlincolnonline.org/lincoln.html
The website of *Abraham Lincoln Online,* a large collection of online resources, including news and a calendar of contemporary Lincoln events, timeline of Lincoln history, copies of speeches, and classroom resources.

www.lmunet.edu/museum/index.html
The website of the Abraham Lincoln Library and Museum in Harrogate, Tennessee. This site contains links to other Lincoln museums, galleries, state parks, and library collections.

http://besthistorysites.net/index.php/american-history/1800/south-slavery
This site, part of a larger website called *Best of History Websites,* is designed for both teachers and students. It provides links to a wealth of information on slavery in America. Check out profiles of slaves living in both northern and southern communities. Listen to the voices of former slaves in "American Slave Narratives."

www.historyplace.com/lincoln/index.html
The Abraham Lincoln section of *The History Place* website. This site offers an extensive annotated timeline with more than 100 entries and more than a dozen thumbnail photographs of Lincoln.

www.loc.gov/rr/program/bib/presidents/lincoln/related.html
Abraham Lincoln: A Resource Guide is part of a series of online history guides based on the U.S. Library of Congress's fascinating and extensive digital collections. The Lincoln guide features links to stories, photos, and documents related to the life and times of the 16th president of the United States, as well as historical events surrounding his presidency, including slavery, the expansion of the nation westward, and the Civil War.

Index

abolitionists 6, 7, 8, 18, 19–20, 23, 27, 31, 35, 42, 52
Adams, John 6
African-American soldiers 7, 33, 43, 44, 53
Alabama 35, 36
Amendments to the U.S. Constitution
  Thirteenth 7, 44, 49, 50–52
  Fourteenth 55–56
  Fifteenth 55–56
American Colonization Society (ACT) 24
Anderson, Marian 57
Army of the Potomac 38

Battle of Antietam 42
Battle of Cold Harbor 49
Battle of Gettysburg 45, 46
Birth of a Nation 54
blab schools 13
Black Codes 56
Black Hawk War 17
Booth, John Wilkes 54–55
border states 38, 39, 44
Breckinridge, John 34
Brooks, Preston S. 29

Civil War 4, 5–6, 7, 8, 25, 27, 29, 31, 32, 33, 35, 36–38, 39, 41, 43, 45–46, 47, 48, 52, 53, 54, 55
Clay, Henry 12, 14, 19, 22, 23, 24, 26, 27, 29
Colonies, original British 5, 6
colonization 23–24
Confederate army 36, 37, 38, 41, 42, 44, 45, 46, 50, 53
Confederate States of America 4, 5, 32, 35–36, 40, 43, 45, 48, 54, 56

Confederates 37, 38, 39, 44, 43, 45
Constitutional Union Party 34
cotton 9, 40

Davis, Jefferson 36, 45
Declaration of Independence, U.S. 5, 6, 7, 29, 31, 46, 57
Democratic Party and Democrats 19, 21, 26, 28, 30, 34, 47, 39, 42, 48, 50
Douglas, Stephen A. 18, 28, 30–31 33, 34
Douglass, Frederick 8

Dred Scott Decision 31
Electoral College 34
Emancipation Proclamation 5, 14, 33, 39–44, 48, 57
Emancipationists 6, 7, 24, 28

Fifty-fourth Massachusetts Volunteer Infantry Regiment 33
Ford's Theatre 54, 55
Fort Sumter 36, 37
Fort Wagner 33
Founding Fathers 6, 29, 46
Franklin, Benjamin 6
Free Soil Party 26
Frémont, John C. 39

Garrison, William Lloyd 8
Georgia 6, 35, 46, 50, 52
Gettysburg Address 46–47
Glory 33
Grant, Ulysses S. 45, 46, 49, 50, 53
Great Britain 5, 6, 12

Hamilton, Alexander 6

Illinois 15, 16, 17, 18, 19, 20, 21, 22, 25, 28, 29, 30, 31, 34, 35, 40, 50, 56
Indiana 10, 12, 13, 14, 15, 35
Industrial Revolution 9

Jefferson, Thomas 6, 8, 57
Johnson, Andrew 54, 55
Johnston, Sarah Bush 13, 14

Kansas 28, 33
Kansas-Nebraska Act 28, 29, 30
Kentucky 8, 11, 12, 13, 14, 19, 21, 22, 38, 44
King Jr., Martin Luther 57, 58

"lame ducks" 50–52
Lee, Robert E. 37, 45, 49, 53
Lee, William 9
Liberia 23, 24, 26
Lincoln, Abraham
  Bible of 58
  birth of 8, 11, 12, 56
  death of 51, 54–55, 58
  elected President 4, 18, 21, 34–35
  first stand against slavery 19–20
  first term of 7, 36–37
  in Illinois Militia 16, 17
  law career of 18, 21, 25
  and Lincoln-Douglas debates 30–31, 33
  and Lyceum Address 20–21
  money, face on 4, 56, 57
  Mt. Rushmore, face on 57
  and "Peoria speech" 29
  re-election of 47, 49, 50
  second inauguration of 52–53
  self-education of 14, 29, 37

Index

state legislative career of
17, 18, 19, 20, 21, 29
store of 17
U.S. House of Representatives career 21, 22, 24–25
vice-presidential nomination 33
and war powers 40–41
and women's suffrage 19
Lincoln, Edward 25
Lincoln, Mary Todd 20, 21, 22, 26, 51
Lincoln Memorial 10, 56, 57
Lincoln, Nancy Hanks 10, 11, 19
Lincoln, Robert Todd 20, 21, 22, 25, 26, 51
Lincoln, Sarah 11
Lincoln, Thomas 11, 12, 13, 15
Lincoln, Tad 26, 51
Lincoln, Willie 26, 51
Louisiana 14, 35

Maine 27
McClellan, George B. 42, 48
Mexican-American War 22, 23, 24, 28
milk sickness 13, 15
miscegenation 50
Mississippi 35, 36, 45
Mississippi River 14, 18, 45
Missouri 27, 28, 38, 39, 44

Missouri Compromise 27, 28

Nebraska Territory 28
New Orleans 14–15

Obama, Barack 58

Pierce, Franklin 36
Polk, James K. 24

"Radical Republicans" 40
Republican Party and Republicans 30, 33, 34, 47, 49

Sangamon Journal 19, 21
Seward, William 33, 42, 54
Sherman, William Tecumseh 50, 52
Sherman's March to the Sea 52
slave laws 9, 12, 25, 31
slave states 4, 5, 6, 7, 8, 9, 12, 19, 25, 27, 28, 38
slave trade 8
slaves
  and border states 43–44
  as "contraband" 41
  fugitive 38–39, 41
  percent of population 8
slavery
  banned 6, 39
  referendum to phase out 24–25

South Carolina 6, 11, 29, 33, 35, 36
Springfield, Illinois 18, 21, 22, 25, 26
Stowe, Harriet Beecher 8
Sumner, Charles 29

territories, U.S. 5, 24, 26, 27, 28, 29, 31, 33, 35, 38
Truth, Sojourner 43

Union forces (army) 36, 37, 41, 45, 49, 50, 52
  generals of 37, 38, 45, 46, 48
  officers enlisting with Confederate forces 37
U.S. Congress 8, 22, 24, 28, 40, 49, 55
  House of Representatives 21, 22, 36, 49, 50
  Senate 29, 36, 49
U.S. Supreme Court 31

Van Buren, Martin 26

Washington, D.C. 12, 22, 24, 25, 40, 43, 48, 52, 57
Washington, George 6, 8, 9, 56, 57
Whigs 19, 21, 26, 28, 30
White House 32, 42, 51, 58
women's suffrage 19, 25

About the Author

David Press lives in Wisconsin, where he buys, sells, writes, and reads books. He is the author of six nonfiction books for young adults, including a multicultural history of sports. David finds the words of Abraham Lincoln inspirational, especially Lincoln's second inaugural address.